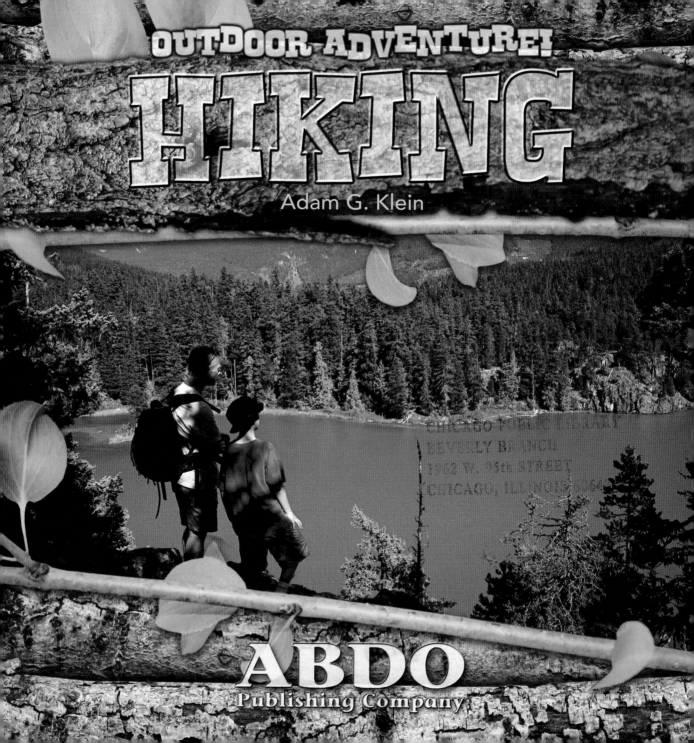

OUTDOOR ADVENTURE!
HIKING

Adam G. Klein

ABDO
Publishing Company

visit us at
www.abdopublishing.com

Published by ABDO Publishing Company, 8000 West 78th Street, Edina, Minnesota 55439.
Copyright © 2008 by Abdo Consulting Group, Inc. International copyrights reserved in all
countries. No part of this book may be reproduced in any form without written permission from
the publisher. The Checkerboard Library™ is a trademark and logo of ABDO Publishing Company.

Printed in the United States.

Cover Photo: Getty Images
Interior Photos: Alamy pp. 28, 29; Corbis pp. 6, 15, 20, 24, 27; Corel Stock Photo Library p. 9;
    Getty Images pp. 1, 9, 10, 14; iStockphoto pp. 5, 7, 12, 13, 16, 19, 21, 22, 23, 25;
    Neil Klinepier pp. 11, 17; Peter Arnold pp. 8, 15, 25, 26

Series Coordinator: Rochelle Baltzer
Editors: Rochelle Baltzer, Megan M. Gunderson, BreAnn Rumsch
Art Direction & Cover Design: Neil Klinepier

Library of Congress Cataloging-in-Publication Data

Klein, Adam G., 1976-
 Hiking / Adam G. Klein.
     p. cm. -- (Outdoor adventure!)
 Includes index.
 ISBN 978-1-59928-959-5
 1. Hiking--Juvenile literature. I. Title.

 GV199.52K54 2008
 796.51--dc22
                              2007029167

CONTENTS

HIKING HOPES

Gabe could hardly sit still in the backseat on the way to his uncle's house. He was especially excited to play in the swimming pool. But the long drive was so boring! So, Gabe was relieved when his father stopped the car at a gas station.

Inside the station, a man and a woman were buying water. Gabe noticed they were each carrying a large backpack and wearing worn leather boots.

Gabe's father asked them if they were heading up the nearby mountain. The couple excitedly told him they planned to hike all the way to the top!

Their enthusiasm made Gabe want to go, too. But, his father said they could hike another time. Gabe was disappointed that he would have to wait. But someday he would return. And just like the couple, Gabe would hike to the top. There, he would stand like a king over the towns below.

A day's hike can lead to beautiful, hidden places. Some of the world's most magnificent locations are only accessible by foot.

WHY HIKE?

Hiking gives us an opportunity to enjoy nature. A hike can be a short day trip on a city trail. Or, it can be a weeklong **trek** through the wilderness. No matter which trail you choose, there will always be exciting things to see!

There are physical benefits to hiking as well. Hiking is good exercise. It is one way to keep your body strong and active. And, getting out in the clean air and the sun can make you feel refreshed. In addition, many people find that hiking relieves **stress**.

Hiking is a fun activity for people of all ages!

The call of adventure also draws many hikers to the trails. A day's journey could lead to a quiet lake. The adventure could continue with the discovery of a hidden cave or jumping fish. You will always find surprises on your travels.

Exploring new paths makes hiking a great hobby. There is nothing like the rewarding feeling of finding your way through the wilderness during your hike!

Some people enjoy hiking in organized groups. Check with the American Hiking Society or local hiking groups for recommendations and hike times.

THE LOCATION

When planning your journey, you must first decide where to hike. Hundreds of national and state parks are scattered across the United States. Most large cities offer hiking trails, too.

Your choice depends on the desired length of your hike. A day trip is the most convenient. Usually, you don't need to travel far to find a trail. Deep caves, rushing waterfalls, or thick forests lie within driving distance of most places. And, many cities have paved, well-maintained hiking trails.

Nature enthusiasts may seek longer trips. For them, hiking the Grand Canyon in Arizona might sound

Many springs in the Grand Canyon contain rare wildlife species that are not found anywhere else in the world.

WATCH FOR LIZARDS ON YOUR HIKE!

appealing. Or, they might enjoy **trekking** the Appalachian Trail. This 2,174-mile (3,499-km) route extends from Georgia to Maine!

The Pacific Crest Trail is another option for serious hikers. This trail stretches along America's West Coast from Canada to Mexico. It is about 2,650 miles (4,265 km) long.

Remember, longer trails are usually less defined. So, hiking them can be challenging. To prepare for any kind of challenge, plan as much as possible before **embarking** on your journey.

Grand Canyon National Park welcomes nearly 5 million visitors each year. Many visitors enter the Grand Canyon on the Bright Angel Trail, which was established long ago by prehistoric peoples.

THE PLAN

A good hiking plan leaves room for enjoyment. Still, every hike should have an estimated time schedule. Before you leave, determine the distance you would like to travel.

For most trails, schedule about two hours to hike one mile (2 km). Then, add ten minutes of rest for every hour of hiking.

People in your group may want to take their time. So, figure in an hour or two for activities that may come up along the way. Finally, don't forget the return trip! It will take some time to get back from an exhausting one-way hike.

Hikers must also plan for changing weather conditions. If the air feels cool, bring a jacket

Hikers must be able to adapt to various situations in the wilderness. You never know what the day may bring!

TIP *It is best to not wear cotton materials on a hike. Knit polyester is a better fabric choice because it dries faster.*

or a sweater. Packing a raincoat is a smart plan. Dressing in layers is also a good idea. That way, you will be prepared for weather changes during your hike. Plan for your journey, but always expect surprises!

PACK THESE ITEMS TO MAKE YOUR TRIP WORRY-FREE AND ENJOYABLE!

- wide-brimmed hat
- extra socks
- rain gear
- sunglasses
- sunscreen
- lip balm

- insect repellent
- first aid kit and book
- pocket knife
- whistle
- map
- compass

- flashlight or headlamp
- camera
- journal and pen
- binoculars
- hand sanitizer
- drinking water

- snacks
- toilet paper
- small sealable bags
  for trash

LONGER TREKS

Hiking for more than one day requires additional equipment. A first aid kit, a map, a compass, and a flashlight or a headlamp are necessary tools.

It is best to pack small, lightweight items. Everything you bring must fit inside your backpack, which should be as light as possible. Remember, you will have to carry your backpack for your entire hike!

There are two kinds of backpacks. Internal-frame packs have supportive metal bars attached to their interiors. They are more compact than external-frame packs. So, hikers carrying them can fit through tight spaces. External-frame packs

Practice map reading and compass reading before embarking on your hike!

have exterior metal bars. These packs sit farther away from the body, keeping you cooler while hiking.

External-frame backpacks allow hikers to stand straighter while walking. However, hikers carrying internal-frame packs are more stable when crossing uneven terrain.

No matter the backpack, find a size that fits you and matches your needs. When wearing your backpack, use both shoulder straps. Buckle the straps around the hips and the chest, as well. This will make the pack fit more securely on your body. And, it will evenly **distribute** the weight of the pack. That way, one muscle group will not carry the entire load.

TASTY TREATS

Hiking requires more energy than the amount your body uses on a normal day. The exercise will probably make you sweat, which also removes **nutrients** from your body. It is important for energy and nutrients to be replaced. So, stop for a snack when you feel a rumble in your stomach. There is no reason to be hungry on a hike!

During a hike, certain foods are better than others. It is difficult to keep fresh foods cold. So, dry foods are best to take along. Peanuts, energy bars, meat jerky, or dried fruits add necessary nutrients back into your body.

Dehydrated meals are a good choice because they don't spoil. And, they are lightweight and easy to make. Hikers can purchase them from special companies. Or, they can dehydrate their own foods at home.

Adults can burn about 2,500 to 4,500 calories per day while hiking. That's 1.5 to 2.5 pounds (.7 to 1.1 kg) of food!

TRAIL MIX

There's a reason trail mix has long been the most popular hiking snack. Its high-energy ingredients keep hikers from tiring. This delicious snack is easy to make. Just follow the recipe below! Use your favorite kinds of nuts and dried fruits to make your own creation!

MIX TOGETHER

1 cup mixed nuts   1/2 cup dried cranberries

1/2 cup sunflower seeds   1/2 cup raisins

1/2 cup M&M's   1 cup granola

(makes about four servings)

DRIED FRUITS

FOLLOW THESE STEPS TO DRY YOUR OWN FRUITS. ASK AN ADULT TO HELP YOU.

1. Cut your favorite fresh fruits into slices about 1/8 to 1/4 inch thick. Place them on a cookie sheet.

2. Heat slices in an oven at 140 degrees Fahrenheit for 6 to 10 hours, depending on the thickness of the slices. Keep the oven door slightly open. Dried fruits should look leathery, and there should be no moisture inside them.

3. Allow the fruits to cool for 30 to 60 minutes.

4. Store dried fruits in glass jars at 60 degrees Fahrenheit or cooler.

WATER

Drinking plenty of water is always important. But, it is especially necessary when you are hiking. Becoming **dehydrated** on a trail is dangerous. So, packing about a half gallon (2 L) of water per day is a good rule. In hot or dry places, bring even more.

It is best to take small, frequent sips of water instead of gulping water every couple of hours. That way, your body is better able to properly use the water.

A small plastic pouch called a water bladder makes taking frequent sips more convenient for hikers. The pouch sits inside of a backpack with an attached hose that reaches outside of the backpack. Other hikers prefer to carry water in bottles inside their backpacks or on a hip belt.

On a trail, you may find water fountains or pumps. Other times, you may come upon lakes, streams, or ponds. But even clear water might be unsafe to drink. It could contain

MAYBE YOU WILL SPOT A BUTTERFLY!

bacteria that your body is not used to.

There are several ways for hikers to **purify** the water they find on a trail. They can boil it for at least three minutes. Or, they can add purification chemicals, such as iodine, to the water. Another option is to use a water filter to remove bacteria. In any case, avoid sickness by making sure water is clean before drinking it.

Don't wait until you feel thirsty to stop for a water break. This is a sign that you are already mildly dehydrated.

CONSERVATION

"Pack it in, pack it out" is a common saying in the wilderness. That means whatever you bring on a trail must also leave with you. Small, sealable bags work well to store garbage until you can dispose of it. Littered food wrappings, leftovers, and other materials destroy the **environment**. They are also a danger to wildlife. Preserving plants is equally important. Certain plants are critical for the survival of animals. And some plants take a long time to grow, so hikers should never pick them. To prevent **foliage** from being ruined, stay on the trail. The animals will appreciate it, and so will other hikers on the path.

Observing nature is fascinating. But, remember to leave objects where you found them to preserve the environment.

Another unavoidable hiking topic is going to the bathroom. This will happen to you or someone in your group, so don't worry about it. Away from the trail and about 200 feet (60 m) from any water sources, dig a hole about six inches (15 cm) deep. When you're finished, cover the hole and camouflage it with leaves.

Do your part to protect the world's beautiful places so that future hikers can experience adventures like yours!

TRAIL MANNERS

Respecting others is important in any situation. In the wilderness, there are several things to keep in mind. People like to spend time in nature because it is peaceful. Loud noise can ruin their experience. Noise can also bother animals. However, this does not mean you can't have fun. There are plenty of ways to enjoy nature without being noisy.

Walking single file on a trail limits damage to the trail and the surrounding ecosystems.

To respect both nature and fellow hikers, you should also know and follow trail rules. For example, people hiking uphill have the right-of-way. This is because hiking uphill is usually more difficult than going downhill. When you are heading downhill, you may see

WHAT TYPES OF ANIMALS WILL YOU SEE?

Many people consider hiking to be a peaceful, quiet activity. Summiting a mountain or reaching an outlook is a great feeling!

hikers coming from the opposite direction. Be sure to step aside and let them pass.

You should also give the hikers in front of you plenty of space. This way, they can enjoy being alone if they wish. Every trail may have different rules. So, check ranger stations and guidebooks for additional rules and tips about hiking **etiquette**.

WILD ANIMALS

There are many kinds of animals to see in the wilderness. Depending on where you hike, you could spot anything from beavers to birds to bears! Observing animals in their natural **environment** is exciting. Each animal has an individual personality that makes it fun to watch.

Binoculars help hikers see animals from a distance. Playing a game of "I Spy" with fellow hikers is a fun way to observe the environment.

Wild animals take care of themselves, and they are healthiest when they hunt their own food. Feeding them leads to trouble. If you offer wild animals food, they can soon become pests. Even harmless creatures such as squirrels and deer might become **aggressive** if humans feed them.

However, some animals are naturally more **aggressive**. Snakes, bears, cougars, mountain lions, and many other creatures live in the wilderness. Usually, these types of animals are scared of people and stay away. But sometimes, they may approach you. This is more likely to happen if your food is visible or left behind on a trail. Then, animals quickly discover that you might have yummy snacks for them. Clapping your hands and making loud noises usually scares them away.

Wild bears rely on natural foods, such as berries and fish. Bears that are fed human food will begin to depend on it. They will likely become aggressive toward humans to obtain it.

STAY SAFE

Just like on any adventure, unfortunate incidents can occur during a hike. It is easy to sprain an ankle if you stumble over a fallen tree branch. Bee stings or snakebites can also happen. And, you can get a **rash** from touching certain plants.

However, there are ways to prevent these events. Before your journey, it is helpful to read about the plants and animals you may encounter. And, packing a first aid kit and book is necessary. This will help you treat cuts, bites, or sprains.

To shield the eyes from sun and wind, you should wear **UVA-** and **UVB**-protective sunglasses. Hikers should also wear sunscreen with an **SPF** of at least 15.

Certain plants are dangerous to touch. For example, contact with poison ivy causes a severe skin rash for many people.

TIP *Check yourself for ticks after hiking in thickly wooded areas. Wear long-sleeved, light-colored clothing and tuck your pants into your socks. This will help keep ticks away and make them easier to spot. If you see a tick on your skin, immediately pull it off with a tweezers.*

A first aid kit helps in minor accidents. First aid kit basics include bandages, gauze pads, athletic tape, moleskin, scissors, tweezers, safety pins, pain relievers, and hand sanitizer.

Sunscreen is most effective when applied every two hours. And, insect repellent helps keep away pesky bugs.

In addition, hikers should always travel in groups. That way, someone will be there to help in case of an accident. If you're hiking near a city, it is fairly easy to get assistance. But in remote places, helicopters are used to rescue people. The chance that something will go wrong is slim. But, it is smart to prepare yourself as best as you can.

ENJOY!

Hiking with others is a great outing. It gives you a chance to spend time with people who share your interest in the outdoors. And, you can experience nature firsthand as you explore the wilderness. It doesn't matter what your reason is for going on a hike. The best reason might even be "just because."

It is best to stretch after a hike, when your muscles are warm. Be sure to hold each stretch for at least 30 seconds.

Remember that as a hiker, you will enter areas where many plants and animals live. It is important to respect their homes. Leave behind only footprints.

Whatever your reason is for venturing into the great outdoors, nature is there for you to enjoy. There are flowers to smell and streams to splash in. Nature can be thrilling. Just like the couple Gabe saw, you could hike to the top of a mountain one day. So get out there and have fun!

GLOSSARY

aggressive - displaying hostility.

aluminum - a light, soft, metallic element that is used in making machinery and other products.

bacteria - tiny, one-celled organisms that can only be seen through a microscope.

dehydration - the result of too little water. When used or lost fluid is not replaced, a person becomes dehydrated. To dehydrate a food, the water is removed from it.

distribute - to position so as to be properly divided and shared throughout an area.

embark - to make a start.

environment - all the surroundings that affect the growth and well-being of a living thing.

etiquette - good manners or polite behavior accepted by a society.

foliage - the leaves of one or more plants, especially growing leaves.

nutrient - a substance found in food and used in the body to promote growth, maintenance, and repair.

purify - to make or become pure.

rash - a breaking out of the skin with red spots.

SPF - sun protection factor. A classification of the U.S. Food and Drug Administration of the degree to which a sunblock or a sunscreen will protect the skin from sunburn.

stress - a physical, chemical, or emotional factor that causes bodily or mental unrest and may be involved in causing some diseases.

terrain - the physical features of an area of land. Mountains, rivers, and canyons can all be part of a terrain.

traction - friction between a body and the surface on which it moves, enabling the body to move without slipping.

trek - a slow, difficult, or complex journey.

UVA - ultraviolet radiation that causes tanning and contributes to aging of the skin.

UVB - ultraviolet radiation that is primarily responsible for sunburn, aging of the skin, and the development of skin cancer.

WEB SITES

To learn more about hiking, visit ABDO Publishing Company on the World Wide Web at www.abdopublishing.com. Web sites about hiking are featured on our Book Links page. These links are routinely monitored and updated to provide the most current information available.

INDEX